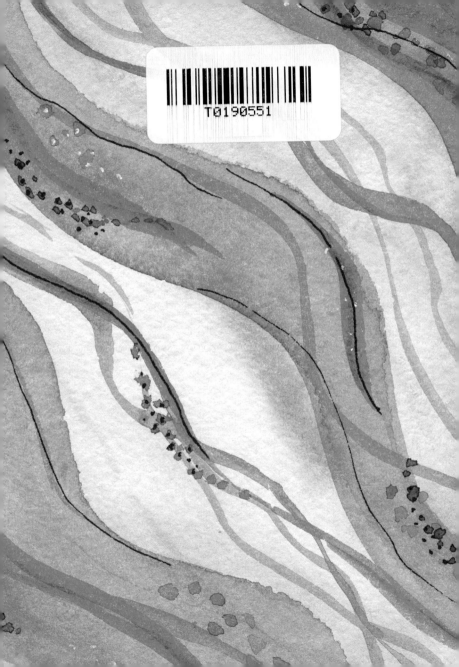
T0190551

Weird is Beautiful

HarperCollins*Publishers*
1 London Bridge Street
London SE1 9GF

www.harpercollins.co.uk

HarperCollins*Publishers*
Macken House, 39/40 Mayor Street Upper,
Dublin 1, D01 C9W8

First published by HarperCollins*Publishers* 2022

10 9 8 7 6 5 4 3 2

© HarperCollins*Publishers* 2022

Liz Marvin asserts the moral right to be identified as the author of this work.

Illustrations Shutterstock.com

A catalogue record of this book is available from the British Library.

HB ISBN 978-0-00-851787-8

Printed and bound in the UAE

All rights reserved. No part of this publication may be reproduced, stored in a retrieval system, or transmitted, in any form or by any means, electronic, mechanical, photocopying, recording or otherwise, without the prior written permission of the publishers.

MIX
Paper | Supporting responsible forestry
FSC™ C007454

This book is produced from independently certified FSC™ paper to ensure responsible forest management.

For more information visit: www.harpercollins.co.uk/green

Weird is Beautiful

THE WISDOM OF
Octopuses

is

HarperCollins*Publishers*

'IT'S WEIRD
NOT TO BE
WEIRD.'

JOHN LENNON

CONTENTS

INTRODUCTION

Think like you've got nine brains, feel like you've got three hearts and hug like you've got eight arms

'WHAT MAKES YOU DIFFERENT OR WEIRD, THAT'S YOUR STRENGTH.'

MERYL STREEP

As any octopus will tell you, it's cool to be different – and it's even better to be weird. Being strange is a superpower, as it unlocks all sorts of experiences and talents you might otherwise never have known you had. Not sure? Read on and let the clever and mysterious octopus convince you to embrace your inner weird.

These squishy-bodied molluscs are capable of amazing physical feats. They can lift up to 40 times their own weight and have a sharp and powerful beak that can deliver a dose of potent venom. If you've ever been on the receiving end of an ink attack, you'll know they are not to be messed with: octopuses know how to stand up for themselves if they have to and they don't let anyone push them around. In other words, this is one invertebrate who doesn't lack backbone.

But these awesome attributes don't represent who an octopus really is. They may be powerful but for them,

aggression is an absolute last resort. Rather, they are constantly curious about everything around them, very intelligent and incredible problem solvers. They are very house-proud, too – they know how important it is to have a den that's comfortable and cosy, where they feel safe. And, more than anything, they are very wise. Which is no surprise when you consider that they have been around since before the dinosaurs. That's given them a lot of time to learn how to navigate a world that's full of wonder and beauty but one that can also be scary and confusing. Octopuses are the ultimate experts on living life on their own terms.

They come in all shapes and sizes, too – from the tiny Octopus wolfi, who is only 2 centimetres long, to the mighty giant Pacific octopus, who proudly weighs in at up to 70 kilograms. But they never compare themselves to other octopuses. Though modest by nature, they are confident in their abilities and happy in their own skins. Independent and unconventional, they do things their own way and they don't care what anyone else thinks.

Life, like the ocean, isn't an easy place to navigate: there are sharp rocks and currents that can threaten to pull you off course. A predator may be around the next corner or a naughty wrasse might be waiting to steal your dinner. Keeping your wits about you is important and sometimes you will need to focus on your own survival.

But life is also full of the magical, the fascinating and the strange, and if we're constantly rushing from rock to rock, chasing after the next crab, or hiding away in our dens, fearful of what might be lurking, then we will miss out on so many wonderful things. Octopuses offer us a masterclass in camouflage and self-protection, but also show us how to appreciate what's around us and celebrate our individual talents.

When can you allow the currents of the ocean to sweep you along and when should you stick your suckers firmly to the rocks and resist? How can you sift through the flotsam and jetsam of life to find the pearls (or the tasty scallop)? When should you show your true colours and when is it a good idea to practise a little self-care and protect yourself? We may never be able to do eight things all at the same time like the octopus, but if we listen carefully to everything they have to teach us, then we will learn the answers to these questions and more.

So let's take a deep dive into the magical and strange world of the octopus. And along the way, we will be inspired to think more wisely, feel more deeply and love unreservedly; after all, no one can hug quite like an octopus can. Wisdom begins in wonder: and there is no creature so weird and wonderful as the octopus.

QUIZ: HOW OCTOPUS ARE YOU?

Before we immerse ourselves in the curious underwater world of these enchanting eight-armed creatures and the wisdom they have to offer, let's start by finding out how in touch you already are with your inner octopus. Are you an ingenious invertebrate who loves solving problems and adapting to new situations, with a whole host of clever tricks up your sleeve(s)? Or are you more of an ocean gadabout, who could do with taking some time to slow down, tending to your den and appreciating that there can be great strength in squashy, skeleton-less vulnerability? Circle the answer that most applies and find out just how octopus you are.

Q1. DO YOU LIKE TO SPEND TIME BY YOURSELF?

a) It's OK, I guess, but I like to know there are others near by. I wouldn't like to go on holiday alone, for example.
b) Maybe a bit too much sometimes. I've very self-sufficient and happy in my own head.
c) God, no. I'm really sociable and know *loads* of people. Even if I don't always remember all their names . . .

Q2. WHAT DOES HOME MEAN TO YOU?

a) I love being at home! It's cosy and comfy and I'm not that interested in going out. I'd hate to have to move.
b) I feel at my best when I have a calm, ordered environment to come back to, but I'm not very tied to one place – wherever I lay my hat . . . !
c) Well, I know this set of keys in my pocket must be for something but, to be honest, I'm hardly ever there! And when I am, it's usually just to change and go out again. I'm not very house-proud.

Q3. HOW GOOD A PROBLEM SOLVER ARE YOU?

a) OK, I guess, although I sometimes panic when something goes wrong and I don't know how to fix it.

b) I've never met a problem I didn't want to solve! I love figuring out how to do new things.

c) Urgh, I usually can't be bothered. If something breaks, someone else can fix it.

Q4. WHAT'S YOUR ATTITUDE TO RISK?

a) 'Danger lurks around every corner' is my motto. I'm very cautious.

b) 'Nothing is truly gained without taking risks' – but it's important to know your limits.

c) 'If you're not living on the edge, then you're taking up too much space!' You've just got to go for it and screw the consequences.

Q5. DO YOU LIKE TRYING NEW THINGS?

a) Not really. I pretty much have the same sandwich for lunch every day.

b) Yes, particularly if it gives me the opportunity to develop my skills or learn something new.

c) Love it! I'm always after the next new, shiny thing. Can't remember when I actually finished something I started, though . . .

Q6. HOW COMFORTABLE ARE YOU WITH BEING VULNERABLE?

a) Not very. I have a tendency to hide in my shell and not let others see the real me.
b) You have to have boundaries, but when you put yourself out there, you can find out a lot about yourself and others.
c) Completely. I depend on a big group of friends for support and will tell anyone anything, really.

ANSWERS

Mostly As: You are currently more hermit crab. You have a tendency to stay indoors in your carefully chosen shell. With a bit of octopus wisdom, you'll learn how to get curious about the world around you, as well as accepting yourself in all your wonderful weirdness.

Mostly Bs: You are well on the way to embracing octopus life! You are adventurous and self-reliant, but calm and comfortable in your own mantle. You will find lots in these pages to relate to and that will help you celebrate your unique, unusual self.

Mostly Cs: You are an anchovy. You generally feel the need to keep moving from one thing to the next and are happiest when part of a big group. Learning to think more like an octopus will help you to know when it's good to go with the current and when it's time to burrow into the seabed and take some me time.

SMART IS
SPECIAL

THE FREEWHEELING BABY OCTOPUS

Octopuses develop their independent and freedom-loving attitude from birth. When they hatch, their parents aren't around to help them and they are too small to swim much, so the tiny larvae drift in the ocean's currents until they are big enough to make a home of their own on the seabed. They join the thousands of minuscule plants and animals that make up what's called phytoplankton – a magical but little understood world on which our oceans depend – with no idea where they might end up.

'WHY FIT IN WHEN YOU WERE BORN TO STAND OUT?'

DR SEUSS

OCTOPUS WISDOM

The next time you hear someone say dismissively, 'That's just a drop in the ocean', remember that a drop of ocean can contain many tiny creatures and plants that are drifting around our planet. What is an inconsequential splash of water to a human eye is actually a whole world in miniature.

TIME TO SETTLE DOWN

As the baby octopuses grow, their arms get longer, they gain their water jet power and they become ready to start the next stage of their lives on the seabed. Wherever they end up once they eventually reach the bottom, that's where they'll have to make their home.

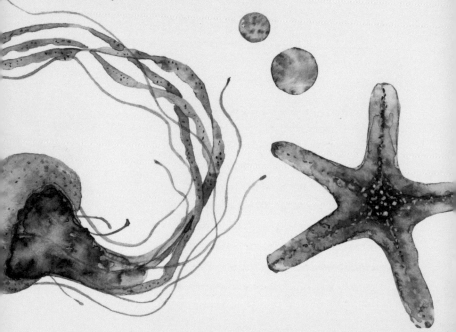

OCTOPUS WISDOM

The wise octopus knows that however much the tides and currents may buffet them when they are young, it's all part of the journey to the place where they will eventually settle and call home.

LIFE AT A CRAWL

Octopuses swim by breathing hard through their gills and pushing out water through their siphon – like their own personal jetpack. Human scientists think that this is quite hard work for an octopus (it even briefly stops one of their three hearts), which is why they prefer to crawl along the seabed. But octopuses know that there are lots of strange and interesting things to find at the bottom of the sea, and those who try to zoom through life at a breakneck pace always end up missing out.

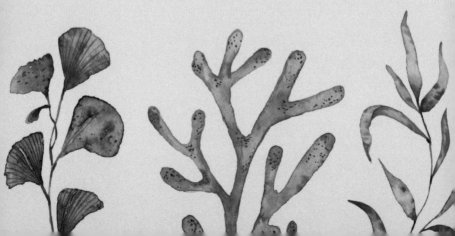

WHAT'S ON YOUR SEABED?

Next time you are out for a walk or waiting for a bus, make a conscious effort to notice what's around you. It's too easy to go past things in a rush without really taking anything in, particularly when you're somewhere very familiar to you. But that way you can miss the little, interesting things that can capture your imagination.

- Start with what's at your feet: are there plants growing through the cracks in the pavement? Can you spot any local wildlife – any creepy-crawlies?
- What about your immediate vicinity? What colours are the front doors of the houses? How many different sorts of trees can you see?
- Is there anybody near you? What are they wearing and where might they be going?

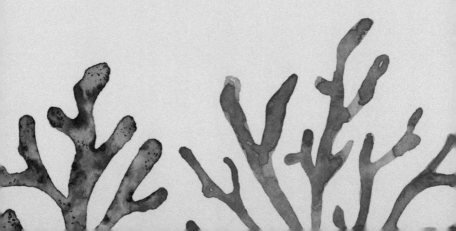

STRENGTH IN VULNERABILITY

The octopus is a mollusc – just like a snail or a clam. But the very big, obvious difference is that an octopus does not have a shell. At some point in their evolution, octopuses ditched their protective armour, leaving them vulnerable to predators. Not having a decent hard hat to hide under has some pretty serious disadvantages, of course, but the amazing opportunities this opened up mean it was more than worth it. Octopuses can squeeze through the tiniest gap, and they can use their jet propulsion to move quickly through the water, their brilliant camouflage skills to fool predators and prey and – most importantly – their intelligence and natural curiosity to help them live their best lives.

OCTOPUS WISDOM

If you hide away in a shell all the time, you'll miss some of the amazing opportunities the ocean has to offer. Don't be afraid to take a risk.

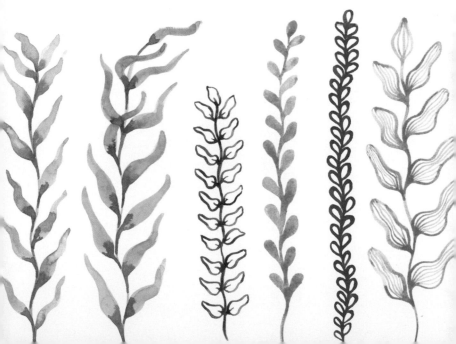

A DEN OF ONE'S OWN

There's no getting away from it – octopuses are pretty solitary animals. They have no desire to hang out, to network, to go to parties. They are content with their own company. Some may go through their lives hardly ever encountering another octopus. But it's not because they are moody or intolerant; we know that if they have to, they can get along, as divers have spotted multiple octopuses living in close proximity in places where housing is at a premium – for example, in shipwrecks on sandy patches of the ocean floor where there aren't many options for suitable dens. It's just that, ideally, they prefer their own space.

OCTOPUS WISDOM

If you find it restful to take some time away from others, then there's no need to apologise for that – embrace your inner octopus and hole up in your den for a spell while you recharge.

LOOKING
AFTER YOUR DEN

We could all learn a lot from the octopus's proactive
and pragmatic attitude to making a house a home. They
move from den to den regularly, but they don't wait
for the perfect place to crop up – they get stuck right
into the DIY. Not only are they efficient housekeepers,
fastidiously taking out the rubbish and dumping it outside
in a trash heap called a midden, they're also happy to take
on some renovation work. If the entrance is too large,
they'll block it up with stones and shells, and they have
also been seen using their water jets to clear out sand to
make their den deeper.

COULD YOU BE MORE OCTOPUS AROUND THE HOUSE?

Got a leaky tap? A wonky table? A picture that still hasn't made it onto the wall? Stop putting it off and bring your den up to octopus standards. Grab some tools and check out YouTube videos if you're not sure how to fix something. It's harder to feel relaxed and content if your immediate environment is messy. The octopus says: you deserve a comfortable home.

OCTOPUSES OR OCTOPI? AND WHAT ABOUT OCTOPODES?

It's tempting to use 'octopi' as the plural of octopus as it's shorter and sort of fun to say. But it's not technically correct. The word 'octopus' comes from Greek *oktōpous*, which means eight feet – slightly confusingly as octopuses don't have feet. Only some words ending 'us' that have come to English from Latin still use an 'i' at the end to make a plural – like cactus/cacti or fungus/fungi. Some pedants have argued for 'octopodes', as that's in keeping with the Ancient Greek way of forming the plural but, really, that's just silly.

Octopuses don't care. As they are creatures who are content in their own company and generally hang out alone, they don't often need a word to refer to more than one of them anyway. If you try to have a conversation with an octopus about the correct way of saying 'more than one octopus', they will just give you a tiny, eight-shouldered shrug.

(And if you were wondering about the word 'cephalopod', it's also Greek and, rather prosaically, means 'head foot'. It's a category of marine mollusc and includes the octopus's cousins, the squid, the cuttlefish and the nautilus – which looks a little like a large, flamboyant prawn.)

THE TEENY, TINY *WOLFI*

The world's littlest octopus is the *Octopus wolfi*, or star-sucker pygmy octopus. They only grow to 2.5 centimetres, but that's OK – small can be mighty, too. They live all over the Indo-Pacific, from the Red Sea to Hawaii, and they like to hang out in warmer, shallower waters. They have excellent eyesight, and their diminutive size means they can go unnoticed by predators, who often just swim on by, leaving them in peace.

OCTOPUS WISDOM

It doesn't matter if you're big or small, the queen of the deep or the prince of the rock pool: embrace what you have and celebrate what makes you you.

PART OF THE COMMUNITY

Octopuses may live alone, but that doesn't mean that they are misanthropic recluses. We know that they can be very tolerant of others in their undersea community. For example, giant Pacific octopuses often find themselves sharing their space with the brightly coloured wrasse fish, who will pop along to see what leftovers might be going spare when the octopus has finished dinner. Some octopuses are not averse to snacking on a hermit crab from time to time, but if one stops by to check out an octopus's midden pile for a new shell because they are looking to upsize, they will often be left in peace.

OCTOPUS WISDOM

The octopus knows that while we're all different, everyone is just trying to live their life and – so long as it's not a mean moray eel who's come calling – it's good to get along.

IS IT WORTH IT?

Getting stuff done efficiently without expending too much energy is a real priority for octopuses, particularly those who live in cold places where life has to happen at a slower pace and wasting resources is very unwise indeed. So there might be a delicious-looking clam near by, but if it's going to take a whole lot of time and effort to crack it open, it might not be worth the bother. Likewise, if that crab is seriously speedy, is it really worth using lots of jetpack energy to catch up with it? So next time you are running around, feeling exhausted, yet not achieving very much, take a moment to ask yourself: what would a deep-sea octopus do?

WHAT'S DRAINING YOUR TANK?

Take stock. Is there an area of your life where you're putting
a lot of effort in but getting little reward? That might be a
friendship that's become too much like hard work, a hobby
you're not really enjoying any more or maybe it's time to
look for a new job. Can you make a change?

41

THE OCTOPUS MIND

While poor, simple vertebrates only have neurons in their brains, two-thirds of an octopus's neurons are in their arms (and they are *not* called tentacles, by the way; octopuses find this common mistake a little annoying). This means that, in essence, each of their eight arms has its very own brain and can work independently. For humans, every tiny bit of information we capture from our surroundings has to go to our brains for processing and every tiny decision has to be made there. But for an octopus, these brain 'outposts' can get on with instantly processing all the information they are able to get from the receptors in their very sensitive skin, without having to bother the main brain with every little detail.

OCTOPUS WISDOM

The octopus shows that there's more than one way to be brainy. Considering that humans only have one brain each, it's amazing how we use them to think in different ways. So instead of stressing about things you find challenging, focus on what your brain is good at and really see what it can do!

WHY ARE OCTOPUSES SO CLEVER?

Octopuses are the smartest molluscs. Now, this might not sound like much, as the competition includes snails and clams* but they are even cleverer than plenty of mammals, too. Being able to actively learn, figure out how to solve problems and remember that information is incredibly useful and probably how the 300 species of octopus that we know about have adapted so well to live in all the different environments that they do. But this level of intelligence is very rare in the animal kingdom. So how did octopuses evolve to be so clever? They probably know, but we have no idea.

*With no offence intended to either. Snails have a great sense of humour and clams are, of course, renowned for being happy, but neither species is realistically going to apply for *Mastermind*.

OCTOPUS WISDOM

Octopus intelligence is a great
reminder to people not to be so
human-centric in the way they see
the world. After all, our ancestors
only go back 6 million years, whereas
the oldest known octopus fossil
lived some 296 million years ago.
Octopuses likely figured out how to
use tools long before humans did.

DIFFERENT
IS
INGENIOUS

'IF YOU ARE ALWAYS TRYING TO BE NORMAL, YOU WILL NEVER KNOW HOW AMAZING YOU CAN BE.'

MAYA ANGELOU

THE POWER
OF EIGHT

To creatures who are not so blessed in
the arm department, eight can seem like
a lot. But being different in this way brings
with it certain superpowers and means that
octopuses can do things other animals can only
dream of. Thanks to each arm having its very own
brain, octopus arms can move in an almost limitless
number of ways independently of each other, and they
can even smell, too. They can use a couple of them to
open a shellfish, while others are feeling around on the
seabed for some more. You could say that this makes
octopuses the best multitaskers in the world.

CAN YOU MULTITASK LIKE AN OCTOPUS?

With our relatively few limbs, we humans will never match an octopus for getting lots done at once, but here's a test to find out how you compare to our cephalopod friends. Start at the top and work your way down, seeing how many things you can do at the same time:

- Pat your head
- Rub your tummy
- Stand on one leg
- Wink with one eye
- Sing a song

Too easy? OK, now try rubbing your head, patting your tummy, hopping, winking with the other eye and singing the song backwards!

FLEXIBLE LIVING

Octopuses have a lot to teach us about adaptability. Not only are they found in all the world's oceans – from the lovely, warm shallows of the Caribbean to underwater canyons in the seriously chilly Bering Sea – but individual octopuses are very resourceful about where they make their dens. They are not interested in real estate with an impressive square footage; however, they do like somewhere boutique and cosy, where all their suckers can make contact with all surfaces in case a predator decides to try to drag them unceremoniously out. For this reason, they also like a small entrance they can just squeeze through. In some muddy, sandy areas of the sea floor there's not much choice, so they have to take what they can get – and this can even include things that we humans have very rudely disposed of into their ocean home. Red octopuses have been known to make their dens in beer bottles, drainpipes and shoes, while some rather grand octopuses in the Mediterranean live in sunken Roman galleons.

OCTOPUS BOOK CLUB

Octopuses don't get much time to read (plus books don't last that long underwater). But here are a few of their favourite classics:

- *War and Plaice* – Leo Tolstoy
- *The Grapes of Wrasse* – John Steinbeck
- *I Capture the Cuttlefish* – Dodie Smith
- *Harry Sea Otter and the Deathly Shallows* – J. K. Rowling
- *To Kill a Moray Eel* – Harper Lee
- *Brighton Rockpool* – Graham Greene
- *The Camomile Prawn* – Mary Wesley
- *Tristram Clamdy* – Laurence Sterne
- *Octo Zhivago* – Boris Pasternak

MOLLUSCS AT THE MOVIES

The octopus community was very pleased to see the sensitive and nuanced characters of Pearl (a flapjack octopus) and Hank (an East Pacific octopus) in Pixar's *Finding Nemo* and *Finding Dory*. Because, frankly, octopuses feel that they have often been misrepresented in popular culture. There's Ursula, the sea witch in *The Little Mermaid*, who is decidedly octopus-like, and supervillain Dr Octopus, one of Spiderman's most challenging adversaries in the Marvel comics. And then there's the monstrous Kraken that first appears in *Pirates of the Caribbean: Dead Man's Chest*, vengefully dragging ship and crew into the depths. Octopuses know that humans find the mysteries of the ocean quite scary, but they did think that was a little much.

OCTOPUS WISDOM

There's no need to be afraid of things just because we don't yet understand them. The octopus says: there is nothing to fear except fear itself. (And sperm whales.)

CHANGE IT UP

Octopuses may be happiest in their own company, but that doesn't mean they like to stick to the same routine. Although many octopuses would say crabs are their favourite food, they still eat a wide and varied diet. And, of course, they are always upping and moving house – partly because it's good to move on if you've eaten most of the food in the immediate vicinity, but also because they enjoy a change of scene. It's unknown whether octopuses are familiar with the human phrase 'a change is as good as a rest', but they would certainly agree.

TRY SOMETHING DIFFERENT

Getting stuck in a rut is no good for our creativity, energy levels or overall enjoyment of life. Sometimes, all it takes is a small, new thing to change it up a bit and make you feel energised and engaged. If you're feeling flat, see how many of these mini challenges you can tick off in a week:

- Start a conversation with someone you've never spoken to before.
- Go exploring – walk or cycle somewhere you haven't been before.
- Cook a dish you've never made.
- Listen to a different genre of music to what you usually go for. So if hip hop is your go-to, try some classical; if you're a rock fan, find some 1960s Motown.
- Ask your friends what their favourite films are and pick the one that seems most different to your usual tastes to watch.
- Learn three new words – in any language you like!

WALK LIKE A COCONUT OCTOPUS

Octopus ingenuity and creativity knows no bounds, and humans are still learning about all the clever things these creatures can do – some of which are admittedly more unorthodox than others. For example, coconut octopuses wrap six of their arms around their bodies while delicately tiptoeing across the seabed on the other two. Whether this impression of a drifting coconut successfully hides the true identity of the octopus, bamboozling its predators, or whether the local viperfish are just laughing too hard to chase after them is unknown, but it obviously works.

OCTOPUS WISDOM

Octopuses aren't afraid to risk looking silly sometimes – and nor should you be. Don't be scared to give it a go. Who cares what others think if it gets results?

PROBLEM SOLVERS

With their incredible dexterity, curious minds and fearsome intelligence, it's no surprise that octopuses have been banned from most TV game shows for being too good. There really is no defeating them. For example, an octopus living in an aquarium in Santa Monica, USA, decided that, while its tank was suitably watery, the ground outside where the visitors walked seemed a little . . . well, dry. So it waited for everyone to go home and set about dismantling the water-recycling system at the top of its enclosure, flooding the place with 200 gallons of seawater. Much better!

AN OCTOPUS BRAIN-TEASER

Answer: see page 128

THREE HEARTS

You know that feeling when you see someone you like and your heart 'skips a beat', or something scares you and you feel your heart pounding? Well, imagine that instead of one heart you had three, like an octopus – that would be pretty intense. Biologically speaking, an octopus has one heart to circulate the blood around the body and another two to pump it past their gills, so they can breathe. But perhaps this is also a sign of what empathetic and deep-feeling creatures they are. Octopuses are very clever decision makers and problem solvers, but they are very sensitive, too.

ARE YOU MORE OF A HEAD OR HEART ANIMAL?

HEAD

You like to make decisions by looking at the evidence and carefully weighing up the options.

HEART

You are guided by your intuition and by what feels right.

You're really good at solving problems in everyday life, but sometimes struggle to know how to help someone you know who's sad.

Your friends laugh at you for being impractical, but they always know they can come to you with a problem.

When you first meet someone, it takes you a while to get to know them.

You often find out someone's entire life story within minutes of meeting them and make friends quickly.

You love action films and thrillers.

Sad films leave you weeping for hours afterwards – but you watch them anyway.

Any worries you have are mostly centred around money, work or the health of those you love.

You are desperately concerned about the plight of bees, whether your friend is upset you didn't text back and that dog you saw outside a shop looking sad.

MASTER CRAFTERS

With their amazing motor skills, helped by all those tiny, pinching suckers, octopuses are the ultimate crafters. Not only do they create new dens on a regular basis, they are masters of the fine art of getting into particularly tight shells. They could use their impressive strength to pull the shell apart, but they often use the more subtle technique of carefully digging into it with their radula – or scrapy mollusc 'tongue' – and using their venom to help dissolve it. It's a real craft as a mussel shell is different to that of a clam, for example, and, as such, needs a different approach. But the octopus always knows what to do and patiently works at their project for as long as it takes.

CRAFTING LIKE AN OCTOPUS

Crafting is a great way to unwind and develop new skills. You'll need to embrace your inner octopus to find the time and really focus (and you might wish you had some extra arms, too), but getting in touch with your creative side is hugely rewarding. Have a look around your home – do you have any old furniture that would be perfect for upcycling? Why not take apart some broken jewellery and see if you can make something entirely new? Or check out some online tutorials and see if you can pick up a whole new crafting skill.

LARGE AND IN CHARGE

Octopuses know that sometimes you've just got to own your space. While they can squish themselves through a tiny gap, lots of them also have the ability to puff themselves up, making them look bigger. They can add to the illusion by basically putting on a mask: they change the colour of their skin around their eyes, making them look bigger and wider apart – like they belong to a larger animal a predator is much less likely to mess with. Even if the creature sizing them up for dinner hesitates just for a second, it buys the octopus time in which to beat a hasty retreat.

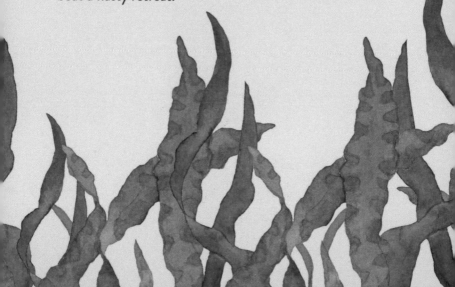

OCTOPUS WISDOM

The octopus says: fake it till you make it. When you're in a sticky situation, sometimes you just have to act bigger and more confident than you feel to help you get through.

SEAGULLS ARE THE THINGS WITH FEATHERS

A poem by Anemone Dickinson

Seagulls are the things with feathers
That perch up top of the sea
And make awful noises without words
That never stop — at all
They need keeping an eye on
Even though they're all the way up there
Those bloody noisy birds
Whose bums I keep seeing
As I've heard it said by many a squid
And on the strangest Sea
That one day, in Extremity,
They might take a bite — of Me.

STRANGE
IS USEFUL

'IT'S EASY TO STAND IN THE CROWD, BUT IT TAKES COURAGE TO STAND ALONE.'

GANDHI

BLUE BLOOD

If you're a mammal reading this, you probably assume that all blood is red, right? Not so. Octopus blood is beautifully blue. Human blood relies on haemoglobin – which contains iron – to transport oxygen around the body, whereas in octopuses, this job is done by hemocyanin, which contains copper molecules, making it blue. Octopuses need quite a lot of oxygen in their blood, which is potentially a bit of a challenge when you live at the bottom of the ocean. So this solution is perfect, particularly because they often need to be able to survive at low temperatures, at which haemoglobin would stop working. After all, octopuses can't migrate somewhere else if the weather turns bad, but they know that if you can't change something, you have to find a way to get comfortable and work with what you've got.

ARE YOU A POIKILOTHERM?

Octopuses don't spend energy on keeping themselves at a constant temperature like mammals do. This means that in cold water their metabolism slows down and they do everything that bit more leisurely. So if someone is nagging you to get out of bed on a cold winter's morning and you just can't seem to get moving, tell them you're not lazy, you're just being a poikilotherm.

OCTOPUS SELF-CARE

Having lots of arms covered in hundreds of suckers that work as tiny pincers is great when it comes to grooming, and octopuses are fastidious in making sure they are always immaculately turned out. It's not about appearances, though (octopuses are so busy being clever and curious about the world that they never consider what others may think of them), but about feeling comfortable and happy in their own skins. Octopuses know that spending some time on looking after yourself in this way sends an important signal to your subconscious that you are worthy of feeling good.

INTRODUCE SOME OCTOPUS PHILOSOPHY INTO YOUR SELF-CARE REGIME

What would make you feel good today? In what small ways can you look after yourself to make it easier to face the world? Remember, it's not about impressing anyone else or trying to look a certain way, but about what *you* need on the inside. Here are some ideas:

- Have a long, relaxing bath while listening to your favourite podcast or album.
- Get your hair cut.
- Reorganise your wardrobe, so all your favourite things to wear are at the front. Take anything that's uncomfortable or doesn't fit right to the charity shop – what's the point in holding on to it?
- Give yourself a home pedicure or facial.

77

TFW . . .
YOU SHED AN ARM

Octopuses have lots of ways of dealing with predators
and they will generally try the simplest tactics first – like
camouflaging until the threat has passed or hiding in their
den. If that doesn't work, they might switch it up and use
their water jet or send a cloud of ink right into the face of
their surprised attacker. But in the stickiest of situations,
when a predator has got hold of them, things are looking
dire and an octopus is almost out of options, there is one
last thing they can do. An octopus has the ability to shed
one of its arms, leaving a confused predator holding a
handful of suckers, rather than the dinner they thought
they'd nailed. It's a painful and extreme tactic that leaves
the octopus feeling sore and wonky for weeks while the
arm grows back, but they will dust themselves down and
be happy they lived to see another day.

OCTOPUS WISDOM

When you've been through a difficult
or bruising encounter, sometimes
the only medicine is time. Our arms
might not grow back, but hearts
heal and scars fade, if we are kind to
ourselves.

SUCKERS

We human animals are very proud of our opposable thumbs. They give us fine motor skills, allowing us to hold pens, tools, etc., and we credit the evolution of our civilisation to being able to pick things up between our fingers and thumbs. However, in octopus terms, this is not very impressive. Every one of an octopus's arms is covered in ingenious suckers that not only allow it to hold tight to pretty much every surface, but also work as tiny pincers, enabling it to pick things up and perform very intricate actions. Plus, they contain sensors, so an octopus can 'taste' with its arms, too. A particularly cool octopus trick is to pass a snack, like a shell or small crab, from one end of an arm all the way to its mouth, like it's on a tiny conveyor belt.

THE STEEPLECHASE-FLOURISH CHALLENGE

This is the nearest we humans can get to an octopus's conveyor-belt trick (you may have seen gangsters in old-fashioned movies doing it):

1. Hold a large coin between your thumb and first finger, palm down, fingers curled under.
2. Now slide it onto the top of your index finger, between the first and second joints.
3. Use the gap between your index and middle finger to flip it over on top of your middle finger.
4. Do the same again with your middle and ring fingers, so the coin moves along to sit on top of your ring finger.
5. Let it slide down the gap between your ring finger and pinky, then use your thumb to push it across your palm and back to the beginning again.

It's pretty tricky, isn't it? If you were an octopus, this would be as easy as opening a clam shell while simultaneously tidying your den.

THE PERFECTLY STRANGE DUMBO OCTOPUS

The very cute Dumbo octopus is the deepest-living octopus known to human scientists; one has even been spotted as far down as 7 kilometres in the Indian Ocean. They have stubby little arms that they tuck underneath themselves and no ink (there's not much point when it's dark). They are named 'Dumbo', slightly meanly, because of two fins – one on each side of their heads – that flap and do look rather adorably like elephant's ears.

OCTOPUS WISDOM

When you're an expert at thriving in places where most other creatures would fear to tread, who cares if someone gives you a silly name? The Dumbo octopus is super-proud of its amazing abilities.

OCTO-PUNDIT

In general, octopuses aren't that interested in sport (though they'd like to try squidditch). But it turns out that they make excellent football pundits. In 2010, Paul, a common octopus, was able to indicate to human staff at the Oberhausen Sea Life Centre that he had a pretty good hunch as to the outcome of Germany's World Cup matches by choosing a mussel from a box with the flag of the team whose victory he foresaw displayed on it. He was spot on seven times and even picked the eventual winner, Spain. This was not a one-off, as Rabio the giant Pacific octopus also correctly predicted the result of three of Japan's matches in the 2018 World Cup.

NOT JUST
FOR PARROTS

It might be hard to imagine that such a squishy creature
is packing a pointy and very hard beak, but they are. It's
hidden in the middle of the octopus, where their eight
arms meet. And not only is it a precision tool for getting
into shellfish, but a deadly weapon, too. The beak can move
like a pair of scissors, and behind it is the octopus's salivary
gland, where the poison is produced, the radula, that acts
like a scraper and the salivary papilla – very small teeth
that work like tiny drills. Quite the Swiss army knife of
nightmares if you are unlucky enough to be octopus prey.

OCTOPUS DANCING

The great thing about having no skeleton whatsoever is that it makes you very flexible – which is great for throwing shapes. Admittedly, managing eight arms without getting in a complete tangle can be something of a challenge, even when each one has its own 'brain'. Some octopuses have been spotted assuming a set of postures called 'flamboyant'; scientists have assumed this is them impersonating seaweed for camouflage and dinner-hunting reasons, but it is, in fact, a popular dance move.

OCTOPUS WISDOM

No matter how many arms you have, remember to throw them in the air like you just don't care once in a while. If you trip over, or find yourself in a bit of a tangle, then just carry on regardless – maybe you'll end up inventing a brand-new dance move.

DON'T MESS WITH AN OCTOPUS

While an octopus much prefers to use their awesome talents creatively to get out of the way of a predator, when push comes to shove, they can certainly assert themselves, using their powerful and sharp beaks, dispensing venom that can paralyse their adversary, and their very strong arms. The beautiful blue-ringed octopus is so poisonous it can even kill humans – although it will try to get away and show its blue rings first, as a warning.

WHAT'S YOUR CONFLICT STYLE?

Do you deal with disagreement like a wise octopus, only getting angry as a last resort, or are you more like a moray eel – inclined to go on the attack? Conflict is a natural part of any animal's life, but sometimes we just have to agree to disagree. Next time you feel yourself getting frustrated or annoyed with someone else's behaviour, try to take a step back, listen to what they are saying and see it from their point of view – even if you still don't like it.

89

GETTING INKED

Of all the tricks an octopus has up their sleeves, this is possibly the coolest. When dealing with a pesky predator, shooting a cloud of noxious ink in its face and using it as a smokescreen to mask their escape has to be the ultimate mic-drop exit. Many octopuses can instantly create an ink cloud much bigger than themselves – with the added bonus that it gets in their adversary's eyes, while also temporarily paralysing their sense of smell. This gives the octopus the opportunity to jet off to safety – though from the predator's point of view, they seem to have simply disappeared in a mysterious cloud of smoke, like the Wicked Witch of the West in *The Wizard of Oz*.

OCTOPUS WISDOM

Don't hang around if a situation is making you feel uncomfortable. Know your boundaries and when to swim away.

SLEEPING WITH THE ANEMONE

Big-brained octopuses may be some of the ocean's smartest occupants, but even they sometimes run up against an annoying problem they can't solve. Certain types of hermit crab have struck up a deal with the spiky sea anemone whereby the latter's poisonous spikes keep the crabs safe from hungry octopuses and, in return, it gets to polish off the hermit crab's leftovers. To an octopus, it feels very irritating to get stung in the face when you were expecting a tasty snack. Sort of like realising too late that there's a wasp in your cider.

OCTOPUS WISDOM

There's not a lot to be done about life's small and sometimes undignified inconveniences; you just have to deal with them and move on. As the well-known octopus saying goes, 'When life gives you anemones, make anemonade.'

SO MUCH DEPENDS ON . . .

A poem by William Octopus Williams

So much depends upon
A sea anemone
Looking quite pointy
In front of the tasty Crab

MYSTERIOUS
IS COOL

'THE MOST BEAUTIFUL THING WE CAN EXPERIENCE IS THE MYSTERIOUS.'

ALBERT EINSTEIN

THE FEARSOME KRAKEN

Sailors and fishermen who worked in the cold seas between Norway and Greenland used to be afraid that they might one day encounter a terrifying sea monster with many arms so long it could wrap them around their boats and pull them under. Well into the eighteenth century, scientists believed that this enormous sea creature, usually depicted as a huge octopus (in fact, the word for octopus in German is *krake*) really existed. French naturalist and cephalopod enthusiast Pierre Denys de Montfort even claimed that ten British warships that had disappeared in mysterious circumstances in 1782 had been sunk by a huge kraken. However, it was a hurricane that was responsible for the loss of the ships, leaving de Montford looking rather silly.

No octopuses ever believed the legend of this terrible monster, but every so often, in the deepest, darkest reaches of the ocean, an octopus will glimpse a huge, ominous shape and swear that they saw the kraken. Sort of like some humans are adamant they they've seen Big Foot or the Loch Ness Monster.

COLOUR YOUR OWN KRAKEN

ESCAPE ARTISTS

While there are some disadvantages to being a soft and squishy mollusc who doesn't live in a shell, an undeniable perk is the ability to squeeze through the tiniest of gaps and make Houdini-like escapes. In 2016, Inky the octopus broke out of his tank at the national aquarium in New Zealand and, it's believed, made a break for freedom down a long, thin drainpipe that led directly to the sea. Another New Zealand octopus living in a research facility was discovered to be regularly sneaking into a different tank to eat some crabs before returning to his own. There's just no containing these clever, independent animals.

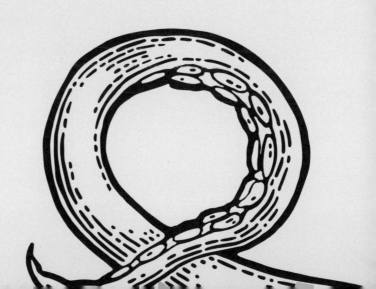

OCTOPUS MAZE

START →

FINISH

OCTOPUS WISDOM

There's a big, wide world out there – so when adventure calls, don't ask permission; be brave enough to seize your chance and make for the open ocean.

OCTOPUS PLAYLIST

Despite not having ears, octopuses are big music fans.*
Here are some of their desert-island discs:

- 'Don't Ink Twice, It's All Right' – Bob Dylan
- 'Living Next Door to Wrasse' – Smokie
- 'The Day We Caught the Crab' – Ocean Colour Scene
- 'Hold Me in Your Eight Arms' – Rick Astley
- 'Get Ur Beak On' – Missy Elliott
- 'Squids in America' – Kim Wilde
- 'I Love Rocks and Sole' – Joan Jett & the Blackhearts
- 'Livin' On a Pier' – Bon Anchovy

*Surprisingly, perhaps, most octopuses do not really
like the song 'Octopus's Garden' by the Beatles. Mainly
because they're not into gardening and they think the
lyrics lack emotional depth. Their feeling is that Ringo
should have stuck to playing the drums and narrating
Thomas the Tank Engine.

CAMOUFLAGE EXPERTS

Now, octopuses aren't annoyed by this, as such, but they are surprised that chameleons get so much credit for simply being able to change colour. To them, this seems pretty basic. After all, octopuses who live in shallower waters (it's less of an asset when you live in the dark!) can not only change their colour in the blink of an eye, they can also add spots, bars and rings and adopt fine gradations of colour to match whatever they are sitting on at the time. They can also use tiny muscles to make little bumps, called papillae, on their skin, to change its texture. And do you know what's even more amazing? Octopuses are colour blind. So how do they know how to mimic the colour of seaweed or a rock? We don't know and they're not telling. It's just one more thing that makes them so magical and mysterious.

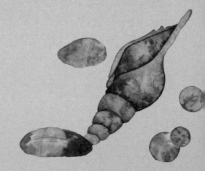

OCTOPUS WISDOM

We all have different skills and talents, but it's important to focus on what you *can* do rather than what you can't. Find your own unique way to accomplish whatever it is your heart(s) desires.

AND THE ACADEMY AWARD GOES TO . . .

With their incredible flexibility, colour-changing abilities and brilliant creativity, octopuses are the ocean's triple threat. These talented method actors can play the role of seaweed, a rock or even another animal to get themselves out of trouble or allow them to sneak up on their prey. They totally inhabit the role to make a predator think they are something completely different.

OCTOPUS WISDOM

It's important to be true to yourself, but that doesn't mean you can't learn from others. So many people we encounter in life have the potential to teach us something interesting or useful if we pay attention and allow them to do so.

THE MARVELLOUS MIMIC OCTOPUS

The Meryl Streep of the underwater world, this amazing octopus can convincingly take on the part of a variety of other creatures, changing body shape as well as colour in a pitch-perfect performance that leaves predators scratching their heads. And they know their audience, too – when they are being bothered by a damselfish, for example, they will hide in a hole, poking out just two of their arms to look like a sea snake, the animal most likely to make a damselfish turn tail and run. Mimic octopuses have also been known to play the role of a jellyfish, a lionfish, a crab and Margaret Thatcher.

111

PASSING CLOUD

When in full camouflage on the seabed, an octopus doesn't want to blow their cover, but they may want an opponent who has disappeared from view to move, and so give away their own location. The strategy they use is called a 'passing cloud'. While still maintaining their disguise, they quickly darken a patch of their skin, as if a cloud has passed across the sea overhead. This appearance of movement can often be enough to make an unfortunate and skittish crab reveal where they are.

OCTOPUS WISDOM

Don't be a nervous crab – be a clever octopus. Change can feel scary, but more often than not, it brings interesting opportunities.

DO OCTOPUSES DREAM OF ELECTRIC EELS?

In 2019, a diver making a documentary who snuck up on a slumbering octopus was amazed to see the octopus change colour as they slept. This could only mean one thing – the octopus was dreaming! That octopuses dream was news to humans, though not, of course, to octopuses. However, being solitary creatures, they hadn't realised that they changed colour while they were asleep, as there's no one else in their den to tell them. The octopus in question was mainly just pleased that the nosy cameraman hadn't caught them snoring.

WHAT DO DREAMS MEAN? AN OCTOPUS'S GUIDE

According to octopus lore, dreaming about certain objects or situations can provide clues to what's going in our subconscious. Have you dreamed about any of these things recently?

- Turning up somewhere in the wrong camouflage – you are anxious about an upcoming event
- Getting stuck in a rock crevice – something is making you feel trapped
- Being chased by a giant crab – you need to face your fears
- Cuttlefish – you are being too rigid in your approach to something*

(*Cuttlefish are famously stubborn and inflexible.)

LOOKING FOR AN INVISIBLE OCTOPUS

Scientists had wondered about the mysterious glass octopus for a hundred years. Based on, well, 'bits' they had discovered in the stomachs of octopus predators, they were pretty sure that somewhere out there lived an octopus who was almost completely transparent. But no one had ever seen one (which makes a lot of sense, if you think about it). However, in 2021, an expedition off the remote Phoenix Islands, about halfway between Papua New Guinea and Hawaii, reported two encounters. It's thought that this octopus lives anywhere between 200 and 3,000 metres beneath the surface in the largest ocean on earth and only its eyes, optic nerve and digestive tract are opaque. You can't help but think they did quite well to find it.

OCTOPUS WISDOM

The glass octopus goes to show what an amazing and special planet we live on, containing creatures beyond our wildest imaginings. All the more reason to take care of our beautiful blue and green home.

SONNET 18
SHALL I COMPARE THEE?

A poem by Krilliam Shakespeare

Shall I compare thee to a Humboldt squid?
Thou art more lovely and less gelatinous.
Rough waves do shake the coral beds,
And a cephalopod's life hath all too short a date.
But your beautiful colour-changing skin shines,
Turning from rock-coloured to yellow to navy;
By chance, or because you're cleverly
impersonating a sea snake;
With your arms, so long and wavy.

But the vagaries of the ocean are many,
And while we enjoy bountiful crab and clam and snail,
We know that around the very next corner,
There might be a bloody enormous sperm whale.
But so long as you can ink,
and your beak stays so pointy,
Your eyes will continue to sparkle,
and remain beautifully bulgy.

FINDING LOVE

Though octopuses are very happy with their fairly solitary lifestyle in the main, the one area where this could cause a problem is when it comes to finding a mate. Because, ultimately, everyone wants to be loved, even when they live at the bottom of a very chilly ocean. But despite the fact that some octopuses spend much of their lives rarely seeing another of their own kind, they still somehow seem to manage to find each other. We don't know how – it's yet another octopus mystery – but they do.

OCTOPUS WISDOM

Never give up looking for someone to love – there may be plenty of fish in the sea but there's one octopus for everyone.

AND IN CONCLUSION: WEIRD IS BEAUTIFUL

'IT IS NOT OUR
DIFFERENCES
THAT DIVIDE
US.

IT'S OUR INABILITY TO RECOGNISE, ACCEPT AND CELEBRATE THOSE DIFFERENCES.'

AUDRE LORDE

The truth is that we are all weird in our own unique ways – and that's what makes each of us special. The octopuses know that understanding and celebrating this is the path to true happiness. And they hope that they have inspired you to embrace your inner octopus – with as many arms as you have at your disposal.

The wide ocean can be scary and it's important to face the risks cautiously but without fear. Don't hide away in your den but appreciate the wonders of the seabed beneath your feet. You may be squishy, but you are tough. Don't waste precious energy on things that drain you and offer little reward. Value your skills, whatever they are, and don't be afraid to look silly from time to time. Dance like you are impersonating seaweed and never stop being curious.

But most of all don't be afraid to be you. Not everyone understands how much beauty there is in all that's strange. Some people are scared of difference. The octopus says: that's not your problem. Now go forth and be weird.

OCT-
KNOWLEDGEMENTS

The octopuses would like to thank Liz Marvin for all her help in transcribing their wisdom. And everyone at HarperCollins for publishing it.

Liz Marvin is not an octopus. She is a writer and editor who lives by the sea on the south coast of England.

Oh, and the answer to the brain-teaser on page 61 was indeed 34. You clever thing! (Did you say 54? I'm afraid that's incorrect, as the BODMAS/BIDMAS rule says you need to multiply first then add. There is always more to learn from the wisdom of octopuses!)

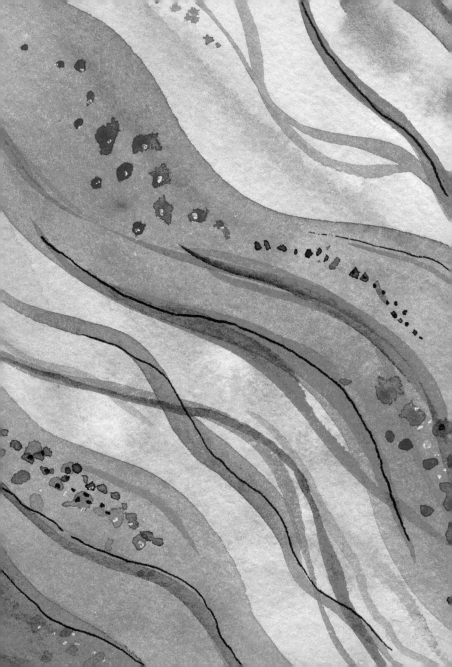